FAMILY AND CONSUMER SCIENCE LIFEPAC 8
FINANCIAL FREEDOM

CONTENTS

Author: **Marcia Parker, M.Ed.**
Editor: Alan Christopherson, M.S.
Illustrations: Alpha Omega Graphics

Alpha Omega Publications®

804 N. 2nd Ave. E., Rock Rapids, IA 51246-1759
© MM by Alpha Omega Publications, Inc.   All rights reserved.
LIFEPAC is a registered trademark of Alpha Omega Publications, Inc.

FINANCIAL FREEDOM

What is financial freedom? Financial freedom is the state of being debt free; it is a state in which a person has his finances in order and keeps them that way. Although you may have a house mortgage or some other long-term credit purchase, you should never get behind in your payments or spend more money than is available. We are commanded to "owe no man any thing..." (Romans 13:8).

Most young people spend a good portion of their lives preparing for adult careers, but they devote little effort to learn how to deal with the monetary rewards of that career. Money needs to be managed or it can be easily wasted. It is very possible to lose some of your hard-earned money without realizing it through poor investment decisions. It is important for you to know how to budget your money for use now, and also to know how to save or invest your money for use later. As teenagers, you may need money to pay for school supplies, dating, entertainment, and putting gas in the car. As young adults, you may need money for rent, food, and education. As older adults, you may need money for a child's education, to buy a vacation home, or to enjoy a comfortable retirement. The trick to managing your money is finding a way to accomplish all of these goals.

We all desire to be financially free.

Of course, the first step to managing money is to have money to manage. The first section of this LIFEPAC® will guide you in applying for a job. You should be able to fill out a job application form, create an impressive résumé, and present yourself effectively during a job interview.

Once your income has been established, learning to handle your finances in a profitable and mature fashion is important. Keeping neat and accurate records, being informed of banking procedures, and realizing available investment opportunities will equip you with the information to help you create a good working personal budget. In order to plan for future expenses as you grow into adulthood and independence, a working knowledge of credit records, insurance plans, and income tax filing will be of great value to you.

The last section of this LIFEPAC will discuss legal matters that can affect your financial stability such as bills of sale and **lease** agreements. Understanding contracts and legal forms is important for the various business transactions that you may make during your lifetime. Although you may not be thinking about your own will, a living will, or what a durable power of attorney is, you may need to be familiar with these documents in the future as they apply to or concern other older family members.

OBJECTIVES

Read these objectives. These objectives tell you what you will be able to do when you have successfully finished this LIFEPAC.

When you have finished this LIFEPAC, you should be able to:

1. Understand the process of filling out a job application form.
2. Prepare your own résumé.
3. Understand the correct procedures for a job interview.
4. Distinguish between descriptive, financial, and combination forms.
5. Describe ways to care for, protect, and store important records.
6. Identify types of banks and banking services.
7. Complete a signature card, endorse checks, and complete deposit slips.
8. Write checks, enter checks in a check register, and reconcile the bank statement with the check register.
9. Identify different types of accounts and other investments.
10. Identify personal values and goals.
11. Determine personal needs and wants.
12. Prepare weekly and monthly budgets.
13. Identify reasons for using credit.
14. Describe types of credit: long term and short term.
15. Develop a responsible attitude toward credit cards.
16. Identify procedures for establishing and keeping a good credit rating.
17. Identify different types of insurance: homeowners, life, health.
18. Identify and understand the use of the most important income tax forms.
19. Understand the legalities concerning bills of sale.
20. Define the following: wills, living wills, and durable power of attorney.
21. Know your rights concerning lease agreements.
22. Identify the responsibilities and legalities involved in purchasing and owning a car.

Note: All vocabulary words in this LIFEPAC appear in **boldface** print the first time they are used. If you are unsure of the meaning when you are reading, study the definitions given in the glossary.

Survey the LIFEPAC. Ask yourself some questions about the study. Write your questions here.

_____

_____

_____

_____

_____

_____

_____

_____

I. GETTING A JOB

The first step to financial freedom is having some source of income. If there is no income, there simply cannot be any spending. Finding a good job, one that is both challenging and interesting, can be a difficult process.

As a teenager, you may not have decided on a career direction yet. However, you do have some ideas of the things that interest you, that you can do well, and that you enjoy. You should realize that you have special talents and strengths in specific areas of intellect. Think about these aspects of yourself. For example, you enjoy and have an aptitude for science and research, you have above average grades, and you are a people person. What are your career options? Doctor, nurse, research scientist, or science teacher are only a few of the choices. If you are outgoing, a good speaker, and enjoy writing, you may consider journalism, broadcasting, public relations, speech teacher, or author.

A job enables us to purchase things we desire.

You may be saying, "How does this affect my job seeking now?" If you are unsure of your career choice, then now is a good time for you to see what the various fields are all about. Seek a position that will give you the opportunity to get experience in a field you may have been considering and to see if it is really something you would enjoy doing for the rest of your working life. If you are sure of your career path, then a job in that field can give added experience and increase your skills for the future.

This section will help you learn how to properly fill out a job application form, prepare your own résumé, and endure and even enjoy that first job interview.

Section Objectives

Review these objectives. When you have completed this section, you should be able to:

1. Understand the process of filling out a job application form.

2. Prepare your own résumé.

3. Understand the correct procedures for a job interview.

The "Help Wanted" sign signals a job opening.

THE APPLICATION FORM

Later on in this LIFEPAC, we will study the different types of forms. All you need to know for this section is that a job application form is a descriptive type of form. Descriptive forms usually answer questions such as: Who? What? When? Where? and Why?

Many employers believe they can learn something about people by studying their job application forms. Is the form neat? Is the writing clear and legible? Is the information written in the right place? If the application is filled out electronically, is the spelling, punctuation, and grammar correct and have all of the fields and questions been completed? Employers look at these things when they are deciding whether to hire someone. Therefore, when completing an application form, be sure to follow the directions given on the form very carefully.

Alpha Omega Publications   Setting The Standard
                                                For Christian Education

application

Name   Laura   Anne   Holt
Address   200 N. Sepulveda Blvd.
City Los Angeles   State CA   Zip 90035
Date 06/22/10   Telephone (310) 555-2206   Social Security # 555-55-5555

Have you previously applied to this company? ☐ yes ☒ no If yes list date(s):
If related to anyone in our employ state name and dept.: Larry Mondello—warehouse
Position applying for Graphic Designer
Are you employed now ☐ yes ☒ no Desired pay open   Date available immediately
Full time ☒ yes ☐ no   Part time ☐ yes ☒ no   Flexible ☒ yes ☐ no
Hours/days: M-F   Willing to work overtime ☒ yes ☐ no
List special training/skills: Proficient in Photoshop and Illustrator. Knows Quark Xpress
In case of emergency notify: Agnes Gooch—neighbor (310) 555-6022
How did you learn of our organization: newspaper ad
Do you speak any foreign languages: Some Spanish

Education	Name & address of school	Course of study	Last year completed	Graduate	Degree or diploma
Grammar	Archie Leach Elementary School	basic	2001	yes	diploma
High	Millard Fillmore High School	college prep.	2005	yes	diploma
College	Cal-State Fullerton	graphic design	2009	yes	BFA
Trade					
Other					

Employment 1 List employers starting with most present or most recent.
Company Ads-R-Us	From 9/08	To 6/10
Address 1234 N. La Cienega Los Angeles	Telephone (310) 555-4321	
Job title Graphic Designer Supervisor M. Donatello	Salary:Beginning $8.00/hr Ending $9.00/hr	
Duties Prepared simple page layouts for supermarket ads	Reason for leaving desire greater challenge	

Employment 2
Company Mr. Slushy's Drive-In	From 6/06	To 9/08
Address 1060 W. Addison, Los Angeles	Telephone (310) 555-1234	
Job title Carhop Supervisor R. Cunningham	Salary:Beginning $5.50/hr Ending $6.00/hr	
Duties Took customer orders, made change, prepared food	Reason for leaving found job in my field	

Employment 3
Company	From	To
Address	Telephone	
Job title Supervisor	Salary:Beginning Ending	
Duties	Reason for leaving	

Please describe any experiences or qualifications other than those positions indicated above. Was in charge of my church's bulletin—
Designed the logo, created a layout and wrote some small articles
We may contact the employers listed above unless you indicate those you do not want us to contact.
Do not contact n/a   Company   Reason

Be as complete and accurate as possible.

Complete the following statements.

1.1   A job application form is a _____ type of form.

Answer *true* **or** *false.*

1.2   _____ In deciding whether or not to hire an applicant, employers can only rely on the information given on an application.

Complete the following activity.

1.3   Fill in the application form on the next page as completely and neatly as is possible. Using accurate information about yourself, fill it out as if it were for an actual job.

Alpha Omega Publications

application

Name

Address

City   State   Zip

Date   Telephone   Social Security #

Have you previously applied to this company? ☐ yes ☐ no If yes list date(s):

If related to anyone in our employ state name and dept.:

Position applying for:

Are you employed now ☐ yes ☐ no Desired pay: Date available:

Full time ☐ yes ☐ no   Part time ☐ yes ☐ no   Flexible ☐ yes ☐ no

Hours/days: Willing to work overtime ☐ yes ☐ no

List special training/skills:

In case of emergency notify:

How did you learn of our organization:

Do you speak any foreign languages:

Education	Name & address of school	Course of study	Last year completed	Graduate	Degree or diploma
Grammar					
High					
College					
Trade					
Other					

Employment 1   List employers starting with most present or most recent.

Company	From	To
Address	Telephone	
Job title Supervisor	Salary:Beginning	Ending
Duties	Reason for leaving	

Employment 2

Company	From	To
Address	Telephone	
Job title Supervisor	Salary:Beginning	Ending
Duties	Reason for leaving	

Employment 3

Company	From	To
Address	Telephone	
Job title Supervisor	Salary:Beginning	Ending
Duties	Reason for leaving	

Please describe any experiences or qualifications other than those positions indicated above.

We may contact the employers listed above unless you indicate those you do not want us to contact.

Do not contact   Company   Reason

 Adult Check _____

         Initial   **Date**

THE RÉSUMÉ

In addition to a job application, it is wise to have an effective résumé to give to the employer. It is best if it is sent by mail in advance of your interview, but it can also be handed personally to the employer at the time of the interview.

What is a résumé? A résumé is a **concise** history of your achievements, education, and previous job experiences and skills.

Your résumé should be brief; it should also be easy to read and understand. Use words that are familiar to the reader and that have a universal appeal. It should be **reader friendly**.

RULES FOR WRITING A RÉSUMÉ: [1]

- Use the most general of job titles. This will open your field of knowledge and experience to encompass more job opportunities.

- Do not list a current salary. You do not want to be eliminated from the running because you overestimated or underestimated your value.

- Try to keep your résumé to one page; definitely take whatever measures are necessary to keep your résumé to no more than two pages.

- Your résumé *must* be typed. You may also use the word-processing program on your computer.

- Emphasize your achievements, previous job experience, and skills and education.

There are three standard types of résumés: chronological, functional, and combination. The most frequently used format is the chronological type. It is exactly as it sounds; it follows your work history backward from the current job, listing companies (stores, employers, etc.) and dates, and responsibilities.

May Ellen Farber has graduated from high school and has moved from Eugene, Oregon to Lincoln, Nebraska to attend college at the University of Nebraska. She is seeking employment at the Tiny Tots Day Care Center. She has chosen the chronological type résumé because she wishes to emphasize her experience in the field of child care.

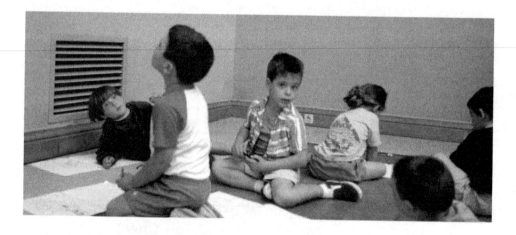

---

1. These rules were adapted from *Knock 'Em Dead* 1997, by Martin Yates, pp 9-10.

MAY ELLEN FARBER

307 S. Washington Street
Lincoln, NE 56008
(506) 555-5722
mfarber@aol.com

PROFESSIONAL EXPERIENCE

Mary's Little Lambs Preschool, Eugene, OR   4/09-5/10
    Supervisor: Mrs. Phyllis Betts
    Child care for children ages 3 and 4. Certified in first aid and
    CPR (Red Cross, 4/99). Leadership in games, crafts, and reading stories.

First Baptist Church, Eugene, OR   5/07-5/10
    Supervisor: Mrs. Janet Brown
    Volunteered in nursery twice a month. Changed diapers,
    bottle fed babies, cuddled, and rocked babies as needed.

Mr. and Mrs. Richard Pyle, Eugene, OR   10/07-4/09
    Baby-sitter for four children, ages ranging from 3 months to 6
    years. Responsible for preparing meals, playing games, reading
    stories, and giving baths.

Mr. and Mrs. Frank Downey, Eugene, OR   5/06-4/09
    Baby-sitter for three children, ages ranging from 4-8. Responsible for
    preparing meals, playing games, reading stories, and giving baths.

EDUCATION:

Eugene High School, Eugene, OR   8/06-5/10
    Health Occupations Class   1/09-5/09
    Home Economics Department—Child Care   8/08-1/09
    Home Economics I, Home Management   8/07-5/08

Red Cross, Certification in First Aid and CPR   4/09

A chronological résumé.

A functional résumé is created without employment dates or company names and mainly concentrates on skills and responsibilities. It can be useful if you have changed careers or when current responsibilities don't relate specifically to the job you desire. Jobs, employment dates, and job titles can be placed inconspicuously at the end.

MAY ELLEN FARBER
307 S. Washington Street
Lincoln, NE 56008
(506) 555-5722
mfarber@aol.com

PROFESSIONAL SKILLS

Management: assistant supervisor of sales in a retail store.
Sales skills: highest sales of the month, three times in one year.
Child care: volunteer work, baby-sitting, and day care assistant in the management of preschool age children: read stories, played games, coordinated crafts, provided meals, and general hygiene care for children.
Skilled in the general care of infants: fed, changed diapers, bathed, rocked, and cuddled infants.
Certified in First Aid and CPR.

PERSONAL ACHIEVEMENTS AND ATTRIBUTES

National Honor Society
Regents Scholarship/Honors College
Class officer 4 years of high school
Captain of Volleyball Team
Plays the piano
Friendly, outgoing, loves children

EDUCATION

Eugene High School, Eugene, OR	8/06-5/10
Red Cross, Certification in First Aid and CPR	4/09

PROFESSIONAL EXPERIENCE

Mary's Little Lambs Preschool, Eugene, OR • Assistant childcare provider	4/09-5/10
Gap for Kids, Eugene, OR • Assistant sales manager	5/08-4/09
First Baptist Church, Eugene, OR • Nursery volunteer	5/07-5/10
Mr. and Mrs. Richard Pyle, Eugene, OR • Baby-sitter	10/07-4/09
Mr. and Mrs. Frank Downey, Eugene, OR • Baby-sitter	5/06-4/09

A functional résumé.

The third type of résumé is the combination type. It is simply, the combination of the chronological and functional résumés. It starts with a brief personal summary, then lists job-specific skills relevant to the position being sought, **segues** into a chronological format that lists the how, where, and when these skills were acquired.

MAY ELLEN FARBER
307 S. Washington Street
Lincoln, NE 56008
(506) 555-5722
mfarber@aol.com

EDUCATION:

Eugene High School, Eugene, OR	8/06-5/10
Health Occupations Class	1/09-5/09
Home Economics Department—Child Care	8/08-1/09
Home Economics I, Home Management	8/07-5/08
Red Cross, Certification in First Aid and CPR	4/09

PERSONAL ACHIEVEMENTS AND ATTRIBUTES

National Honor Society
Regents Scholarship/Honors College
Class officer 4 years of high school
Captain of Volleyball Team
Plays the piano
Friendly, outgoing, loves children

PROFESSIONAL EXPERIENCE

Mary's Little Lambs Preschool, Eugene, OR   4/09-5/10
Supervisor: Mrs. Phyllis Betts
Child care for children ages 3 and 4.
(Red Cross, 4/99). Demonstrated leadership in games, crafts, and reading stories.

First Baptist Church, Eugene, OR   5/07-5/10
Supervisor: Mrs. Janet Brown
Volunteered in nursery twice a month. Changed diapers, bottle fed babies, cuddled, and rocked babies as needed.

Mr. and Mrs. Richard Pyle, Eugene, OR   10/07-4/09
Baby-sitter for four children, ages ranging from 3 months to 6 years. Responsible for preparing meals, playing games, reading stories, and bedtime baths.

Mr. and Mrs. Frank Downey, Eugene, OR   5/06-4/09
Baby-sitter for three children, ages ranging from 4-8. Responsible for preparing meals, playing games, reading stories, and bedtime baths.

A combination type résumé.

9

Answer the following.

1.4   What is a résumé?

_____

_____

_____

1.5   A résumé that lists all of your previous job experiences from most to least recent is a _____ résumé.

1.6   A résumé that concentrates on previous skills and responsibilities is a _____ _____ résumé.

1.7   A _____ résumé combines both the chronological and functional résumés.

Complete the following activity.

1.8   Write your own résumé.

   a.   Follow one of the three formats that have been presented.

   b.   Type the résumé.

   c.   Check spelling, punctuation, etc.   Adult Check   _____

                                                                Initial   Date

THE INTERVIEW

To many applicants, the most frightening part of an interview is the fear of the unknown. When you walk into the room and the questioning begins, you will have more confidence and **poise** if you have some idea of what to anticipate. The following suggestions for proper preparation and decorum during the employment interview should help **dispel** many of your fears. Following these suggestions will give you confidence and may increase your chances of being hired.[2]

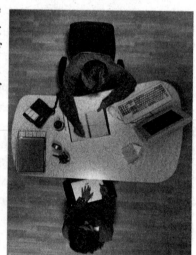

The job interview.

Advanced preparation is the first and possibly the most important step in the interview process. Before you can effectively proceed with an actual interview, you will need to have a number of facts and details at your fingertips. These facts need to be organized in such a way that you will be able to recall them instantly when you need them. If your résumé is done correctly, this will be your best source for this information. You need to be able to recall and verbally give information concerning your education, your achievements, and your work experience.

2. These suggestions are adapted from *The Five Minute Interview*, by Richard H. Beatty.

Learn as much as possible beforehand.

Another area of advanced preparation concerns the place of business or company to which you are applying. Always collect as much information as possible about the company and position before the interview. Today, it is quite easy to obtain such information from the Internet. Do a search of the company's name. You should be able to find an annual report to inform you of the company's financial stability. You may be able to find a description and objectives of the position you desire, and information concerning the company's work ethics. The more you know about the company and position, the more confidence you will feel. Also, this information will tell you if this is a company you would like to work for.

Even in the realm of Christian ministry and employment, it is wise to find out about the reputation and character of the ministry before you go there. It is wrong to anticipate that all ministries function the same way. It is also wrong to think that you will change the ministry. Either you will change to fit the ministry or you will most likely be asked to find a new ministry.

Incorrect

Correct

A good first impression is crucial. The moment we set eyes on someone, our minds quickly make an evaluation and judgment. The same is true for the potential employer whose job it is to assess us. Remember who you are and Who you are representing. "You are a child of the King, created in His image." (Galatians 3:26, Genesis 1:26)

Get plenty of sleep the night before the interview so that you feel fresh and alert.

Eat a nourishing breakfast so you will feel satisfied and have a reserve source of energy. However, don't overeat because this may make you feel tired and sluggish.

Be on time. Being late will start your interview off with a negative impression. Being five to ten minutes early will create a more favorable response from the potential employer. It will also help you feel more relaxed and confident as you enter the interview.

Like it or not, your outward image, your attitude, your confidence level, and your overall delivery are all affected by the clothes you wear. The respect you receive at the interview is in direct proportion to the respect your visual image earns for you even before you speak a word.

Be sure your clothes are clean and neatly pressed. Shoes should be well shined. Avoid wearing outlandish styles or colors. Dress appropriately for the position and organization for which you will be interviewing. In most cases, for men, a dark blue or gray business suit with a white or light blue long-sleeved shirt and an appropriately colored tie will work nicely. Socks should compliment the suit. Be conservative in your accessories; trendy jewelry or child-like watches do not enhance a professional image.

For women, the choice is much broader but should be guided by conservative colors and good taste. Hemlines come and go. While there is some leeway as to what is appropriate for everyday wear on the job, the safest bet for an interview is usually to select a length just slightly below the knee. Suitable colors for a business suit for an interview include charcoal, medium gray, steel gray, maroon, black, and navy blue. All of these look smart with a long-sleeved white blouse. A neck scarf is a very professional looking accessory and can serve as a powerful status symbol. Do not forget pantyhose. Shoes should be leather, brown and black are best, but a woman is safe wearing navy and burgundy. Because a briefcase is a symbol of authority, it is an excellent choice for the female applicant. Do not, however, bring both your purse and a briefcase to the interview. Jewelry should be kept to a minimum. When applying makeup, remember that natural is the key word. Do not appear overly made-up.

Pay attention to personal hygiene and grooming. Hair (including mustaches and beards) should be neatly trimmed and combed. Hands should be clean and fingernails should be neatly filed. Perfume and cologne should be used with moderation and should not overpower the interviewer.

Don't chew gum or eat during the interview. This distracts from your presentation and overall image.

Be polite, courteous, and friendly to the interviewer's support staff (i.e., secretary, administrative assistant, etc.). These individuals often relay their impressions to their supervisor, and may affect whether or not you will get the job.

Extend a firm handshake.

When greeting the interviewer, be pleasant; smile, extend a firm handshake, and look him in the eye. Enter the room assertively. Do not take a seat until the interviewer offers you one.

One's facial expressions can give either a favorable or unfavorable impression to the interviewer. Let your facial expression radiate a confident and relaxed demeanor. Tight smiles and tension in the facial muscles may indicate an inability to handle stress.

Maintain eye contact throughout the interview. Good eye contact shows interest in what the other person is saying. Occasionally look away at appropriate moments so the interviewer does not feel challenged to a staring contest. Your goal should be to maintain a calm, steady, nonthreatening gaze. Frequent looking away or looking down conveys that you are either unfriendly, distant, or that you have something to hide.

Correct   **Incorrect**

Gesticulate appropriately to make a key point. Be careful to not over-gesticulate, distracting the interviewer and drawing his or her attention away from what you are saying. Fidgeting hands can convey nervousness or impatience and can be very annoying. Avoid tapping your fingers, playing with pencils and paper clips, stroking your beard or hair, pulling your ear, rubbing your nose, and so on.

Be aware of your posture. When seated, sit up straight with your bottom well back in the chair. Do not slouch, but lean forward slightly showing interest and friendliness toward the interviewer. It is better not to cross your legs at the knee. Your posture when walking can be important. Good posture can send a message of confidence. Keep your shoulders back straight, maintain an erect posture, smile, and make eye contact when appropriate. Folding or crossing your arms in front of you basically sends a negative message to the interviewer.

If you wear glasses, then wear them. It will not impress anyone if you squint or cannot see well during the interview. If you don't like the way you look in glasses, then consider getting contacts. Never wear dark glasses to an interview. You will seem secretive.

Be pleasant, friendly, and polite throughout the interview. Remember to smile from time to time. You'll want to establish and maintain good **rapport** with the interviewer throughout the discussion. Your smile is a powerful positive body signal. Offer a confident smile as frequently as opportunity allows.

Make sure you turn off your cellular phone and/or pager so there will not be any interruptions during the interview. Keep them in your briefcase or purse.

Be careful not to dominate the interview discussion. Be attentive and respond to what the interviewer's words and body language are communicating.

Take paper and pencil and be prepared to ask questions. Here are some questions that you may want to ask or topics from which you may create your own questions. Some of the following questions or topics will not be applicable to your situation right now, but will be good resource material for your future.

Find out why the job is open, who had it last, and what happened to him. Was he/she promoted or fired? How many people have held this position in the last couple of years? What happened to them subsequently?

Why did the interviewer join the company? How long has he been there? What is it about the company that keeps him there?

To whom would you report? Will you get the opportunity to meet that person?

Where is the job located? What are the travel requirements, if any?

What type of training is required and how long is it? What type of training is available?

What would your first assignment be?

What are the realistic chances for growth in the job? Where are the opportunities for greatest growth within the company?

What are the skills and attributes most needed to get ahead in the company?

Who will be the company's major competitor over the next few years? How does the interviewer feel the company stacks up against them?

What has been the growth pattern of the company over the last five years? Is it profitable? How profitable? Is the company privately or publicly held?

If there is a written job description, may you see it?

How regularly do performance evaluations occur? What model do they follow?

Sample questions to ask at a job interview.

Be prepared to answer questions about your early background, your education, interests, work experience, management effectiveness, and personal effectiveness. Being able to present yourself with confidence and poise in any interview will be an asset all of your life. Not only will you have employment interviews, but you may have interviews for college entrance, one-on-one with professors, volunteer opportunities, etc.

Answer the following questions.

1.9 In what areas will you need to be prepared to answer questions by the interviewer concerning your personal background? _____

_____

1.10 Why should you learn as much as possible about the company for which you are interviewing?

_____

1.11 Why is it so important to be on time for an interview? _____

_____

1.12 If you had to pick one word to describe the way you should dress for an interview, what would it be? _____

1.13 Why is it so important to be polite to the interviewer's support staff? _____

_____

1.14 How should you first greet the interviewer? _____

1.15 Why is it bad to frequently look away from the interviewer or to look down? _____

_____

1.16 Good posture sends a message of _____ .

1.17 Should an applicant bring his own questions to an interview? _____

 Complete the following activity.

1.18 Participate in a mock job interview. Have a parent, friend, or pastor conduct the interview. You will be graded on your appearance, posture, attitude, confidence, and poise. If you are presently looking for a job, this can be an actual job interview.

If possible, videotape the interview. This will enable the student to review gestures, mannerisms, and tone of voice.

To the instructor: There are a number of sources that give excellent interview questions to ask the student for this activity if you need them. The books listed in the bibliography are good sources and you can find some questions through the Internet. Be sure to include questions from the student's early background, education, work experience, management effectiveness, and personal effectiveness. *2000 What Color is your Parachute?*, by Richard Boles, is in its 30th edition. A helpful guide for anyone entering (or re-entering) the job market, this book directs the steps of the applicant in a rather easy-to-read fashion. The new edition also has a companion website.

Adult Check _____

                          Initial   **Date**

Review the material in this section in preparation for the Self Test. The Self Test will check your mastery of this particular section. The items missed on this Self Test will indicate specific areas where restudy is needed for mastery.

SELF TEST 1

Fill in the blanks (each answer, 4 points).

1.01   A job application form is a _____ type of form.

1.02   A résumé that lists all of your previous job experiences from most to least recent is a
_____ résumé.

1.03   A résumé that concentrates on past skills and responsibilities is a _____ résumé.

1.04   A _____ résumé gives the most overall general information.

1.05   You should dress _____ for an interview.

1.06   Good posture can send a message of _____ .

1.07   Greet the interviewer with a _____ handshake.

Answer *true* **or** *false* (each answer, 4 points).

1.08   _____   Employers rely only on the information given on an application form when deciding whether or not to hire an applicant.

1.09   _____   Advanced preparation is the first step in the interview process.

1.010 _____   You do not need to collect information beforehand if applying for a job within a
Christian ministry.

1.011 _____   First impressions are important.

1.012 _____   It is a good idea to be on time or even early to an interview.

1.013 _____   Chew gum or eat mints during an interview so you don't offend the interviewer
with your bad breath.

1.014 _____   Maintain good eye contact with the interviewer, but do not glare.

1.015 _____   Be prepared to ask questions of your own at an interview.

1.016 _____   Dominate the interview discussion so that all your important qualities for the
job are mentioned.

1.017 _____   Looking down or avoiding eye contact indicates to the interviewer that you may
have something to hide.

Complete the following (each answer, 4 points).

1.018 Define résumé. _____

_____

1.019   List two rules concerned with writing a good résumé.

     a. _____

       _____

     b. _____

       _____

Short answer (each answer, 5 points).

1.020   What three areas of your personal life should you be prepared to answer questions about when asked by the interviewer?

     a. _____

     b. _____

     c. _____

1.021   Describe from your perspective (male or female) an appropriate outfit to wear to an interview.

     _____

     _____

     _____

II. PERSONAL FINANCE

Everyone has to manage financial records at some point or another in his personal life. As individuals we maintain personal records for budgets, credits, and banking. As citizens, we maintain records related to state and federal tax reporting. This section will explore each of these aspects of your personal finances.

Section Objectives

Review these objectives. When you have completed this section, you should be able to:

4. Distinguish between descriptive, financial, and combination forms.

5. Describe ways to care for, protect, and store important records.

6. Identify types of banks and banking services

7. Complete a signature card, endorse checks, and complete deposit slips.

8. Write checks, enter checks in a check register, and reconcile the bank statement with the check register.

9. Identify different types of accounts and other investments.

10. Identify personal values and goals.

11. Determine personal needs and wants.

12. Prepare weekly and monthly budgets.

13. Identify reasons for using credit.

14. Describe types of credit: long term and short term.

15. Develop a responsible attitude toward credit cards.

16. Identify procedures for establishing and keeping a good credit rating.

17. Identify different types of insurance: homeowners, life, health.

18. Identify and understand the use of the most important income tax forms.

PERSONAL RECORDKEEPING

All your life you will have to deal with records. For example you will have to fill in job applications and tax forms. You will receive records as well, such as report cards, receipts, and social security cards. You will have to decide where to keep them. You need a system of keeping your records so that you can find them quickly and easily. Also, federal law requires parents, for tax purposes, to fill out forms for Social Security numbers when each child turns six.

Throughout life you will have to fill out forms for one reason or another. Below is a list of some of the forms you will have to fill out to:

Get a job   Withdraw money from a bank
Place an order by mail   Deposit money in a bank
Get a Social Security number   Get a driver's license
Apply to college   Enter a hospital
File an income tax return   Apply for insurance

18

A form is made to help you give complete information. Printed guide words tell you what to write, such as your name and address and where to write it. Forms have spaces or lines for writing the information.

There are three kinds of forms: descriptive, financial, and combination. A descriptive form usually answers the questions: Who? What? When? Where? and Why? Note the advantages of using a form such as the telephone message shown here. The person taking the message knows that the important information will be there and the person receiving the message knows exactly where to find everything.

A financial form deals with money. An example of a financial form would be an order form. It includes catalog numbers, quantities, unit prices, and totals. Note that the form asks for answers to the questions: How much? and How many?

DATE *May 3* TIME *1:30* AM **PM**
TO *Mary Jane*
While You Were Out
M _*rs. Brown*_
OF _*Tiny Tots Daycare*_
PHONE _*(480) 556-7777*_

TELEPHONED	WILL CALL AGAIN
CALLED TO SEE YOU	RETURNED YOUR CALL
WANTS TO SEE YOU	URGENT
PLEASE CALL	VISITED YOUR OFFICE

MESSAGE:
She would like you to work next week on Monday as well as Wednesday.

A descriptive form.

GENERAL ORDER FORM

Item #	Description	Qty.	✔if P/U	Unit Price	Total
Bib 0315	Complete 3rd grade Bible Boxed Set	1		$49.95	$49.95
His 0315	Complete 3rd grade Hist Boxed Set	1		$49.95	$49.95
Lan 0315	Complete 3rd grade Lang. Boxed Set	1		$49.95	$49.95
Mat 0315	Complete 3rd grade Math Boxed Set	1		$49.95	$49.95
Sci 0315	Complete 3rd grade Sci. Boxed Set	1		$49.95	$49.95

Order Taken By/Date _*Marge S.   5/22/09*_

Ship To:

Name _*Mrs. Laura Petrie*_

Address _*15 Bonnie Meadow Ln*_

City _*New Rochelle*_

State _*N.Y.*_   Zip _*01234*_

Phone (_*917*_)   _*555-2541*_

Product Total $249.95
Less Discount $ 7.45
Order Total $242.50

Method of Payment:

❑ Cash   ❑ Check #_____

☑ Credit Card:

☑ Visa   ❑ Master Card   ❑ Discover

Credit Card Number   Exp. Date:
[1888][9922][2266][9888]   6/11

Signature _*Mrs. Laura Petrie*_

804 N. 2nd Ave. E., Rock Rapids, IA 51246-1759   800-622-3070   www.aop.com

A financial form.

A combination form has space for descriptive and financial information. This restaurant receipt asks for descriptive information:

The number of customers	The server's initials
The check number	The table number
The food ordered	The date

At the same time, it asks for financial information:

The cost of each item	The amount of tax
The subtotal	The total cost

Whenever you fill out forms, be sure that you **verify** the information. Double check your work for accuracy.

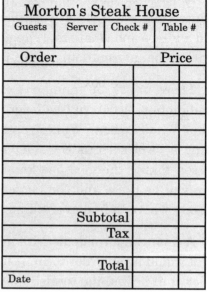

Morton's Steak House

Guests	Server	Check #	Table #

Order		Price	
	Subtotal		
	Tax		
	Total		
Date			

A combination form.

Expandable file

If you are **conscientious**, you will save copies of records such as certificates, diplomas, checks, bank records, licenses, and agreements. If you start organizing your important papers now, it will be second nature to do it as you become an adult. There are several ways to protect records and other valuable items.

An expandable file is a heavy paper folder with pockets that provide places for storing papers. Each pocket has a tab for alphabetic filing or for filing by dates. An expandable file is ideal for storing the following papers:

Warranties and guarantees	Rental leases
Earnings records	Savings account passbooks
Installment contracts	Receipts
School records	Written agreements
Medical records	Canceled checks or bank statements

A record book or financial ledger has pages for recording information. Some examples of information that is best kept in a record book or ledger include:

Lists of insurance companies, policy numbers and amounts, and medical records

Due dates for rent or mortgage payments, installments, and insurance payments

List of banks and savings and checking account numbers

Income tax information, including donations, medical expenses, and business expenses

Employment facts, including names and addresses of companies worked for, dates of employment, and beginning and ending salaries

Date for warranties and guarantees on major appliances, tires, and automobiles

Social Security numbers

Credit card account numbers

List of locations of important documents

A safe deposit box can be rented at most banks for a yearly fee. The safe deposit boxes are located within the bank vault. Only **depositors** whose signatures are on file may enter the vault area. Two keys are needed to open each safe-deposit box. The bank has one key and the depositor has the other key to the box.

Safe deposit box

A safe deposit box provides protection against loss from theft and fire. It is a good place to store valuables such as these:

Savings bonds	Bonds	Stock certificates
Expensive jewelry	Deeds	Mortgage papers
Copies of wills		

Fireproof safes

A good fireproof safe will protect its contents from damage in fires up to 1,800 degrees Fahrenheit. In addition, it can be locked. People often use a fireproof safe to store the following:

Insurance policies	Marriage licenses
Naturalization papers	Passports
Birth certificates	Adoption certificates
Tax records	Spare cash
Jewelry	

Photographs of household furnishings or other valuables (in case of fire)
Receipts for expensive items (cameras, computers, etc.)
Credit cards not carried in wallet or purse
Written agreements and contracts
Title certificates to cars, motorcycles, boats

Answer the following.

2.1   Forms answering questions such as Who? What? When? Where? and Why? are called _____
_____ forms.

2.2   Forms answering questions such as How much? and How many? are called _____
_____ forms.

2.3   Forms answering a mixture of questions are called _____ forms.

2.4   List two reasons for you to fill out forms in your personal life.

a. _____

b. _____

2.5   _____ is the process of checking information for completeness and accuracy.

2.6   A heavy paper folder with pockets for storing papers is called a(n) _____
_____ .

2.7   A locked container that resists heat is a(n) _____ .

2.8   A locked container within a bank vault is a(n) _____.

2.9   Mortgage papers should be stored in a(n) _____.

2.10   Rental leases should be stored in a(n) _____.

Match the terms. Use the best answer for protecting each record. Answers will be used more than once.

2.11   _____ U.S. Savings Bond

2.12   _____ high school diploma

2.13   _____ stock certificates

2.14   _____ last year's tax records

2.15   _____ savings account passbook

2.16   _____ CD player warranty

2.17   _____ list of medical expenses

2.18   _____ earnings record

2.19   _____ list of insurance policies

2.20   _____ birth certificate

2.21   _____ photographs of furnishings

2.22   _____ apartment lease agreement

2.23   _____ marriage certificate

2.24   _____ date for expiration of TV warranty

a.   expandable file

b.   fireproof safe

c.   safe deposit box

d.   record book

PERSONAL BANKING AND INVESTMENTS

Banking is an important activity in your life by helping you keep track of your money and keep it safe. Because banking is a service business, you can expect a friendly welcome there. Banks make a profit by charging fees for services and by collecting interest on loans. Banks offer a variety of services: checking accounts, savings accounts, safe-deposit boxes, traveler's checks, bank credit cards, loans, and ATMs (Automated Teller Machines). You can even bank by phone or over the Internet.

There are several types of financial institutions that can provide a full range of services. We will look at four such institutions.

A bank teller will help you keep track of your finances.

22

Savings banks and savings and loans tend to be small institutions that serve a particular area. Many believe that the service is more personal than one would receive from a large bank. Generally, fees charged for checking and other services are lower than those of commercial banks. Savings accounts are usually insured up to $100,000 by the Federal Deposit Insurance Corporation (FDIC).

Commercial banks offer a full range of banking services. They tend to be large and have numerous branches, with many operating on a global scale. Deposits are insured by the FDIC up to the same limit.

Credit unions are nonprofit organizations that are owned by their members. They offer savings plans, checking accounts, loans, and some even offer home mortgages. Deposits are insured up to $100,000 by the National Credit Union Association. All members of a credit union usually have a common bond, such as a place of employment or union affiliation.

Brokerage firms offer investment services that may include checking and money-market accounts. Many require large minimum balances.

What ever financial institution you choose, you will benefit from having a personal checking account. Checking accounts provide you with the means of paying for purchases without carrying a large sum of cash with you and checks provide an easy way to pay bills by mail.

Opening a checking account is a matter of filling out a form and depositing money to start the account. A signature card shows the official signature of each person opening the account and asks basic information: name, address, phone number, and type of account to be opened (checking or savings; individual or joint). The card also shows the official signature(s) of the account holder(s). The bank uses this signature to verify that checks presented for payment were indeed signed by the account holder(s).

Both cash and checks can be deposited into a checking or savings account. Banks provide easy to complete deposit slips as seen below.

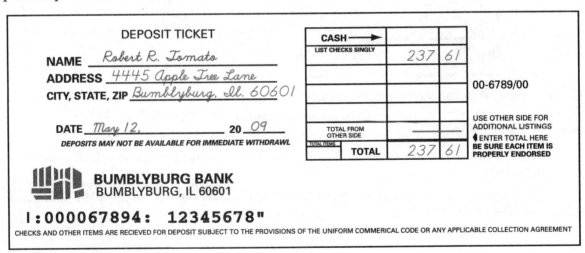

You have two options when you receive a check (e.g., a paycheck). You can sign the check and cash it—the bank will give you cash for the full amount of the check—or you can deposit it into your bank account. In either case, you need to sign the check, and your signature is the endorsement. To endorse a check, turn it over and sign it at the left end.

The check **register** is a book of forms that provide space for writing in the dates, amounts, and payees for all checks. A check is an order to a bank to pay someone money. The **payee** is the person who receives the check. A check register also provides space for deposits.

NUMBER	DATE	DESCRIPTION OF TRANSACTION	PAYMENT/DEBT (−)	✓ T	FEE (IF ANY) (−)	DEPOSIT/CREDIT (+)	BALANCE
		RECORD ALL CHARGES OR CREDITS THAT AFFECT YOUR ACCOUNT					$ 756 | 82
1234	5/10	Bills T.V. & Electronics	125 | 35				− 125 | 35
		new C.D. player					631 | 47
	5/12	Paycheck deposit				237 | 61	+ 237 | 61
							869 | 08
1235	5/12	Stuff-Mart	65 | 58				− 65 | 58
		groceries & misc.					803 | 50
1236	5/13	Bumblyburg Exxon	10 | 00				− 10 | 00
		gas					793 | 50
1237	5/13	Cox Cable of Bumblyburg	27 | 50				− 27 | 50
							766 | 00
1238	5/14	Bumblyburg Church	24 | 00				− 24 | 00
		tithe					742 | 00

REMEMBER TO RECORD AUTOMATIC PAYMENTS/DEPOSITS ON DATE AUTHORIZED.

A portion of a check register.

The best way to write checks and keep the check register is to follow a step-by-step procedure. First of all, always complete the check register before writing the check. Fill in the date, amount, and other information. After you have entered the data in the check register, calculate a new balance to see whether you have enough money to cover the check you are about to write. If you do, then you are ready to write the check, as follows:

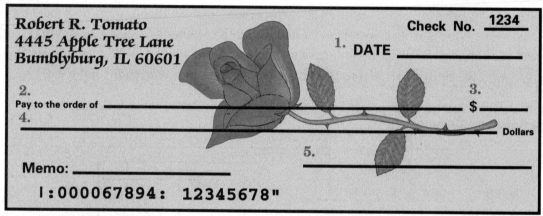

1. Using a pen, fill in the date—month, day, and year. Do not use pencil or erasable pen.
2. Clearly write or print the name of the payee on the line following the words "Pay to the order of."
3. Enter in figures for the exact amount of the check close to the dollar symbol.
4. On the line below "Pay to the order of," write the dollar amount of the check in words (e.g., "fifty-five and").
    a. If the amount is a whole-dollar amount, also write "and 00/100" to indicate "and no cents."
    b. If the amount does include part of a dollar, use figures to write the cents amount—for example 35/100 for 35 cents.

If the written amount differs from the number amount, the bank will use the written amount.

5. Review the check to make sure that the date, the payee, the number amount, and the written amount are correct, then sign the check.

Each check that you write is sent or given to the payee of the check. The payee then cashes or deposits the check. The check is returned to your bank and the amount is subtracted from your checking account balance. An overdrawn account or overdraft results from writing a check for an amount that is greater than the balance in the account. There will be a fine for this oversight. Keeping your bank register up to date will help keep you from making this mistake.

The bank keeps a record of each customer's checking account. This record shows the amounts of all checks written as well as charges subtracted from the account and deposits and interest added to the account. A copy of the bank's records is sent to the depositor each month. This record is called a bank statement.

It is the **depositor's** responsibility to make the check register balance with the bank statement balance. This process is called **reconciling**. Many banks provide a form on which the depositor may prepare the reconciliation. This form is often written on the back of the bank statement and provides easy to follow instructions to help the depositor find the reasons for a difference between the bank statement balance and the check register balance.

Savings accounts have several advantages. First of all, savings accounts earn interest for depositors. Interest is money that banks pay for the use of the depositors' money. Second, savings accounts are safe; banks have special vaults, electronic equipment, and guards to keep money safe. Third, depositing money into or withdrawing money from savings accounts is very convenient.

Savings accounts are available in various types according to the savings needs of the depositor:

A regular savings account is a bank account that earns interest at a fixed rate.

A certificate of deposit (CD) pays a higher interest than a regular savings account but requires a minimum deposit. Further, the money in the certificate cannot be withdrawn for a certain length of time.

A money market account pays higher interest than a regular account and permits withdrawals and deposits, but it requires a minimum balance at all times.

Certificates of Deposit (CD)

Savings, interest-earning checking accounts, money-market accounts, and certificates of deposit are only some of the investment options open to you. You can also put your money in stocks, bonds, and mutual funds.

When you buy a company's stock, you buy a piece of the company. It is possible to make money two ways: the company pays its shareholders (those who own its stock) dividends, which come from the company's profits; or you can sell the stock for a higher price than you paid for it. Of course, neither one of these scenarios is guaranteed.

Bonds are issued by corporations, state and local governments, the federal government, and even government agencies. When you buy a bond you are making a loan to whomever issued the bond. Bonds have an interest rate, which is how you make your money; and a set period of time until **maturity**.

Mutual funds are collections of stocks, bonds, or whatever the investments happen to be. Mutual funds offer some advantages over buying single stocks or bonds. First, the funds are managed by professionals who can adjust the mix of stocks or bonds to accommodate market conditions. Second, your money is spread over a variety of investments, so a single company in trouble will have little impact on your overall fund. And finally, you can invest in some funds for as little as $500.

In his book, *Consider Your Options,* author Kaye A. Thomas, states "...you don't need years of study to be a successful investor. The basics can be set forth in just eleven words: start early, pay debts, buy stocks, diversify, avoid churning, control expenses." (*Start early*) What he is saying here, is that you should start investing as soon as you are financially able to do so. (*Pay debts*) Debts are negative investments, so pay off all your credit cards and get out of and stay out of debt. (*Buy stocks*) Thomas states that stocks have historically been proven to be a better investment than real estate, bonds, precious metals, or collectibles. (*Diversify*) Diversify simply means don't keep all your eggs in one basket; buy more than one or two stocks. (*Avoid churning*) To avoid churning means to avoid constantly buying and selling stocks or mutual funds. Long term investors seem to do better than those who sell frequently. (*Control Expenses*) Expenses can dwindle your returns. Consider the cost of trading and the effect it has on taxes.

Answer the following question.

2.25   How do banks make money? _____

_____

Match the terms with the institution they best describe.

2.26   _____ offers investment services   a.   savings bank

2.27   _____ nonprofit organization owned by its members   b.   commercial bank

2.28   _____ has numerous branches   c.   credit union

2.29   _____ more personal   d.   brokerage firm

2.30   _____ offers a full range of banking services

2.31   _____ members may have same place of employment

2.32   _____ service fees are likely to be lower

Complete the following.

2.33   An order to a bank to pay money is called a(n) _____ .

2.34   The form listing the checks and money to be deposited to an account is called a(n) _____

_____ .

2.35   The form with an account holder's official signature is called a(n) _____

_____ .

2.36   Before a check can be deposited, it should be _____ .

2.37   The person to whom a check is written is called the _____ .

2.38   The booklet of forms used to record written checks and account balances is called the _____

_____ .

FAMILY AND
CONSUMER SCIENCE

eight

LIFEPAC TEST

80 / 100

Name _____

Date _____

Score _____

FAMILY AND CONSUMER SCIENCE 08: LIFEPAC TEST

Choose the best answer (each answer, 4 points).

1. A job application is an example of a _____ type of form.
   a. descriptive
   b. financial
   c. chronological
   d. combination

2. Which of the following is **not** true about writing a résumé? _____
   a. The three standard types of résumés are the functional, chronological, and combination.
   b. The résumé should be typed and four pages long.
   c. The résumé is a concise history of your achievements, education, and previous job experience and skills.

3. Which of the following is **not** true about the interview? _____
   a. Advanced preparation is the first and possibly the most important step in the interview process.
   b. You should be prepared with questions of your own.
   c. You do not need to collect information beforehand if applying for a job within a Christian ministry.

4. Checking information to see if it is accurate and complete is called _____ .
   a. reporting
   b. transposing
   c. verifying
   d. reconciling

5. An account with too little money in it to cover a check the depositor has written is a(n)_____ .
   a. overdrawn account
   b. checking account
   c. regular account
   d. money market account

6. A record of checks, service charges, and deposits that the bank sends to depositors each month is a _____ .
   a. reconciliation statement
   b. bank statement
   c. check register
   d. deposit slip

7. A(n) _____ is the payee's signature on the back of the check.

   a. certification
   b. promissory note
   c. endorsement
   d. overdraft

8. The depositor's written order to the bank to pay out a certain amount from the depositor's checking account is called a(n) _____ .
   a. check
   b. endorsement
   c. receipt
   d. promissory note

9. A plan showing how money is to be received and spent is a _____ .
   a. goal
   b. budget
   c. balance
   d. value

10. An agreement with a store that allows a customer to pay for purchases at a later date is a _____ .
    a. charge account
    b. down payment
    c. principal
    d. interest

11. A fee paid for the use of money is a(n) _____ .
   a. installment plan
   b. down payment
   c. finance charge
   d. interest

12. Payments made every three months are called _____ .
   a. quarterly payments
   b. semiannual payments
   c. triennial payments
   d. monthly payments

13. _____ is **not** included in a bill of sale.
   a. A detailed description of the item
   b. A specific set of rights to the buyer
   c. Signatures of both parties
   d. The make, model, and color of an item

14. A _____ gives your lawyer the right to handle your financial and medical affairs in the event that you are incapacitated.
   a. joint tenancy
   b. living will
   c. durable power of attorney
   d. contract

15. A _____ is most likely to offer investment services.
   a. brokerage firm
   b. savings and loan
   c. credit union
   d. bank

16. A teenager is **least** likely to use _____ when figuring his income tax.
   a. 1040EZ
   b. itemized deductions
   c. standard deduction
   d. W 2 form

17. Stock certificates should be stored in a(n)_____ .
   a. fireproof safe
   b. expandable folder
   c. safe-deposit box
   d. desk drawer

18. The FDIC insures an account up to _____ .
   a. $125,000
   b. $100,000
   c. $150,000
   d. $200,000

19. Group health insurance is _____ expensive than individual health insurance.
   a. less
   b. more
   c. about the same
   d. none of the above

20. Which of the following is **not** true concerning leases? _____
   a. The "access to the apartment" gives the landlord the right to enter your apartment with your permission and with ample notice.
   b. A lease is an agreement to rent land or buildings to another person for a payment for a certain period of time.
   c. It is safe to assume that the utilities will be paid by the landlord.

Short Answer (each answer, 5 points).

21. Explain the statement "maintain good eye contact with the interviewer, but do not glare."

    _____

    _____

    _____

22. Describe from your perspective (male or female) an appropriate outfit to wear to an interview.

    _____

    _____

    _____

Short Answer (this question, 10 points).

23. What should the Christian view of financial freedom be? How can this be accomplished? Use Scripture and/or Christian principles to support your statements.

    _____

    _____

    _____

2.39   When the check amount is greater than the account balance, the check is called a(n)
        _____ check.

2.40   The monthly record listing the checks, deposits, and charges for an account is the
        _____ .

2.41   Making the bank statement balance and the check register balance agree is _____
        _____ .

2.42   What are three advantages of a savings account?

        a.   _____

        b.   _____

        c.   _____

2.43   For the use of depositor's money, the bank pays _____ .

2.44   FDIC insures an account up to $ _____ .

2.45   A savings account that offers a fixed rate of interest is called a(n) _____
        savings account.

2.46   An account that requires a minimum deposit for a certain period of time is called a(n)
        _____ .

2.47   An account that requires a minimum balance yet allows the depositor to deposit more money or
        to withdraw funds is called a(n) _____ account.

2.48   What are three other options for investing your money?

        a.   _____

        b.   _____

        c.   _____

PERSONAL BUDGETING

Financial freedom comes from good money management. Good money management will help you avoid borrowing too much money and will let you save money for the things you need and want. Effective money management does not come naturally or by accident. It takes good planning. It results from careful budgeting.

Values are things that we rate very highly, things that are important to us. Honesty, freedom, education, family, religion, health, and wealth are examples of common values. Values affect a person's goals. Goals are the things we want to accomplish. They are objectives.

The time it takes you to reach a goal will vary depending on the specific goal. A long-term goal may take a year or more to reach. A short-term goal takes less time to achieve. Sometimes a long-term goal is accomplished through several short-term goals.

We all have needs and wants. Needs are the things that we must have. Food, shelter, and clothing are examples of the most basic physical needs. There are other needs that are not as basic as these such as transportation, safety, and education. On the other hand, wants are things that we would like to have or to do. A bicycle, for example, may adequately satisfy your need for transportation to and from school. However, your wants may include a sports car. A mature individual knows how to reconcile the two.

The mature individual can balance his wants and needs.

 Complete the following activity.

2.49   Make a list of your financial goals for a two-week period. Then make a list of your long-term goals. Beside each goal, state a plan for accomplishing this goal; determine how much to save in a designated time period (day, week, month) and how long it will take you to save that amount.

Short term goals:	Long term goals
Example: buy a jogging suit: use earnings from next two baby sitting jobs.	**Example:** College education: $50.00 a month into savings from wages at hardware store job for four years.

Adult Check _____

Initial   Date

A budget is a plan for using your income to meet your needs and wants and to reach your goals. To track your day-to-day activities and earnings, you will need a cash flow statement or chart. This statement can help you develop a budget because it will tell you how much you currently spend and where you need to cut back. It is common to discover you are spending more money than you realized on certain items. This is a good discipline to learn, because you can use the information to adjust your spending habits, such as cutting back unnecessary items and putting more money into savings. A cash flow chart is divided into *income* and *expenses*. See the example below.

CASH FLOW CHART FOR MARRIED COUPLE			
Income	*Yourself*	*Spouse*	*Total*
Salary/wages			
Interest/dividends			
Social Security			
Retirement plans			
Other investments			
Total Income			
Expenses			
Tithe			
Savings			
Income taxes			
Real estate taxes			
Insurance (health, life, car, homeowner's, etc.)			
Mortgage or rent payments			
Utilities			
Auto loans			
Credit card debts			
Other debt payments			
Transportation			
Food			
Restaurants			
Entertainment			
Holiday expenses			
Gifts			
Education			
Clothing			
Personal items			
Other			
Miscellaneous			
Total Expenses			

Although this chart was created for a married couple, you can see the many items that might apply to your own cash flow chart. Of course, you do not have any social security income yet, but you may have other income such as wages, interests, and dividends earned from employment, savings accounts, and checking accounts, respectively. Your list of expenses might include: tithe, school lunches, dating/entertainment, clothing, car payments and/or maintenance, education savings, etc.

Whatever cash flow plan you decide upon, remember that God should receive his portion first. If we are to "be found faithful," (1 Corinthians 4:2) we must be good stewards of God's gracious giving to us. If we're faithful to God, He will be faithful to provide our *needs* and sometimes more (Philippians 4:19). As a Christian, a wise steward of finances will give the first portion, whether it be 10 percent or more to God; the second 10 percent or more should go directly to some savings plan, and the rest should be used for living expenses. If you are saving for college, switch the last two amounts around if at all possible.

Complete the following activities.

2.50   Think of one item you purchase a lot of, such as soda, gum, bottled water, etc. _____ . Figure out how much you spend on this one item over a year's time. _____ Is there an alternative to spending so much on one item? _____ Is this item a need or a want? _____ Are you willing to go without this one item in order to save for a more important long-term goal? _____

2.51   Keep track of your income and expenses for one week and then fill out the cash flow chart accordingly. Your cash flow chart will need only two columns: Income/expenses and total amounts. Do you need to make adjustments in your budget? _____ If so, where and how?

Income/expenses	Total amounts

Adult Check _____

Initial   Date

As you grow into adulthood there will be other things to consider in your financial planning. You should be familiar with the following.

Everyone has a general idea of how Social Security works. The government deducts money from your paycheck, then when you retire after age 65, you receive money back from the government. The income you receive is based on an average of your 35 highest salaried years. The minimum age for retirement is 62, at which time you will receive reduced benefits.

Most Americans retire after age 65.

Many large companies offer some sort of pension plan to their employees. In short, an employer contributes money to an account in the employee's name and when the employee retires he takes the money in a lump sum or receives regular payments.

Another way a company can help with retirement is with a 401(k) plan. You save money two ways with this type of plan: You contribute to the plan, but your contributions remain untaxed until you withdraw the money. In addition, the money you earn on the investment is also tax deferred until you withdraw it.

There are also a couple of plans that you can set up yourself. Individual Retirement Accounts (IRAs) allow you to invest money that accumulates tax free until you withdraw it at retirement. Another option is a tax-deferred **annuity**. In this type of plan you invest with an insurance company.

Answer the following questions.

2.52   At what age does one start collecting Social Security? _____

2.53   List two retirement financial plans that companies offer.

    a. _____

    b. _____

2.54   What are two plans you might set up for yourself?

    a. _____

    b. _____

CREDIT RECORDS

When you apply for a loan or a credit card, the institution that you are borrowing from expects two things: one, that you pay back the amount you borrowed (the principal); and two, that you pay a finance charge for the use of the money.

To determine how dependable you are, the bank will request a credit report from one of the national credit-reporting bureaus. The report is a summary of your financial history. It tells the bank how you have handled loans in the past and your current amount of debt. It is extremely important to keep your credit rating in good standing. Pay off all your debts. Think before you buy. Will you be able to pay for all the purchases you make today, when the bills come next month? Keep all your receipts and check them against the bills you receive.

Credit is the right to buy something now and pay for it later. Short-term credit means that you pay for an item in a short period of time. An example of an item you might buy on short-term credit would be a CD player or a computer. Long-term credit means that you pay for an expensive item over a period of several years. An example of an item you might buy on long-term credit would be a car or a college education. A finance charge or interest is a fee paid for the use of credit. Sometimes you can avoid paying any interest on a short-term credit. For example, if you pay the full amount owed each month on your store charge account or bank credit card, you do not have to pay interest. This is the smart way to handle your finances.

A store charge account is an agreement with a store that allows a customer to buy merchandise and pay for it later. It is one type of short-term credit available. Stores offer different kinds of charge accounts which give customers different methods for paying their monthly charges. The two most popular types are:

Regular Charge Account. Under the terms of a regular charge account, the customer pays the total of each monthly bill within 30 days. The store does not charge the customer any finance charge or extra fees for this type of charge account. The customer pays only for the items purchased and any sales tax.

Revolving Charge Account. The revolving charge account allows the customer to pay the total bill over several months. The customer may pay only part of the total bill each month. The drawback to this plan is that the customer is charged a finance fee.

A credit card issued by a store is used only to charge purchases made from that store. Banks also issue credit cards such as MasterCard®, Discover®, or VISA®. A bank credit card allows a customer to make credit purchases at many different stores and businesses.

Sometimes there are annual fees for this service, depending on the institution from which the card is issued.

Credit cards are protected against loss. If you report the card lost or stolen before it is used by someone else, you cannot be held responsible for any unauthorized use. If the card is used before you report it stolen or lost, you will be liable for up to $50 per card. It is a good idea to keep a list of credit card account numbers and phone numbers in a safe place in case you need to report them missing.

> **A NOTE OF ADVICE:** It is a good policy to never purchase anything on short-term credit unless you know in advance that the money is there to cover it within the 30 days in which it will be due. An unexpected *need* is the only acceptable reason for you to purchase on short-term credit. Why should the bank, store, or lending institution make money from you because you were too impatient to wait to purchase something you *wanted*? Credit cards are a convenient way to pay for purchases, but misusing them carries financial consequences. Credit card interest charges can be very high, and it is wise to avoid having to pay them. Never give your card number to anyone unless you are buying something. Destroy all carbons to keep your card number out of the hands of dishonest people.

Long-term credit is used to buy an expensive item such as a home or a car and pay for it over several years. Long-term credit is usually obtained at a bank, savings and loan, finance company, or credit union. When you borrow money from any of these institutions, you obtain a loan by signing a note. A note is a written promise to repay a loan. It states the rate of interest to be paid and what will happen if the loan plus interest is not repaid.

Loans are made to people who need money now and are able to pay it back over several years. They may need the money for such things as:

A car. Most people cannot afford to buy a car with cash, so they obtain a car loan. Today, there is a second option to consider: a lease. Both options entail making monthly payments over several years. The car lease will also require a large lump sum payment at the end of the lease when the car is returned to the leasing agent.

A home. Nearly everyone who buys a home obtains a loan—called a mortgage loan. A house payment should never total more than one week's salary. The purchase cost should not total more than two-and-one-half times one yearly salary.

An education. To pay for tuition and other educational expenses, one may get a student loan.

One may get a student
loan for college.

Long-term credit is used to
buy a home.

A NOTE OF ADVICE: Make sure that long-term credit or loan is for an appreciable item or an investment in your future. A car may be the exception to this rule, as very few people have the cash on hand to buy a car outright. A house usually increases in value over the years, which makes it a good investment. Borrowing money to go to business school or college, for example, is often a good investment in your future because of the likelihood of increased earnings.

 Answer the following.

2.55 What two things do loan institutions expect from the borrower?

a. _____

b. _____

2.56 What is a credit report? _____

_____

2.57 _____ is the right to buy something now and pay for it later.

2.58 Give an example of a short-term credit. _____

2.59   How can you avoid paying finance charges on short-term credit? _____

_____

2.60   A credit card that can be used to charge purchases at many different stores and businesses is a(n)
        _____ credit card.

2.61   What is a good rule to adopt when considering long-term credit?_____

_____

Complete the following activity.

2.62   Phyllis Black wants to buy a $395 videocassette recorder (VCR). She works full-time at the Central
        Towers Mall where she earns $255 a week. She attends college classes but finds it difficult to
        schedule study time and still participate in social and sports activities.

        Each week, Phyllis spends more than her budget allows, forcing her to borrow $100 a month from
        her parents. She has a $60 dollar furniture payment each month and she often buys on impulse
        during a lunch hour walk.

        The salesperson at Bill's TV Sales is urging Phyllis to take advantage of the sale price of $395 for
        the VCR by signing a purchase agreement for "just $95 down and $30 a month."

        a. Do you think the VCR should be Phyllis' most important goal at this time? Why or Why not?

            _____

            _____

            _____

        b. Are Phyllis' finances in good shape? Explain your answer.

            _____

            _____

            _____

            _____

        c. What should Phyllis say to the salesperson at Bill's TV Sales?

            _____

Adult Check _____
                  Initial   **Date**

34

INSURANCE

Insurance is an important part of everyone's financial plan. Without it, property loss due to fire or some other catastrophe or the serious illness or death of a wage earner, could leave a family penniless. We will look at four types of insurance: car, homeowner's, health, and life. First here are some general terms with which you need to be familiar.

Agent. An insurance agent is the person who sells insurance policies. Some agents work for only one company. Others, called independent agents, offer policies from a number of companies.

Claim. This is your request for payment from an insurance company.

Deductible. This is the amount you agree to pay before the insurance company begins paying on a policy. For example, if you have $500 damage to your car windshield and you have a deductible of $50, the insurance company will pay $450, while you are responsible for the $50.

Endorsement. This is an attachment to a policy that changes the policy's original terms.

Premium. This is the annual amount you pay for insurance coverage.

An insurance agent helps you select a policy.

Co insurance. After you reach your deductible, the insurance company will pay a portion of the bill while you pay the rest, with an 80/20 split—with you paying the 20 percent—being the most common.

One of the responsibilities of owning a car is making sure that it is insured. Most states require that you have car insurance. If you are stopped by a police officer for any reason you may have to show proof of insurance. At the very least, one should have liability insurance in case of an accident. This will protect your financial stability in case the injured party sues you.

The standard homeowner's policy usually covers:

•The house and any separate structure on the property, such as a garage or tool shed.

•Your furniture and other personal possessions. The amount covered is usually 50 percent of the amount of insurance on the building.

•Your liability if someone is injured while on your property.

Homeowner's insurance protects your home and personal possessions.

Health insurance provides coverage when you are sick, need surgery, or have an accident. The least expensive type of health insurance is provided through a group of some sort, such as your employer, a professional association, or a union. You can, however, purchase a policy as an individual. Policies vary widely.

The most common types of coverage include:

- *Hospital-surgical policies* cover conditions that require you to be in a hospital for treatment. Some policies require a deductible, others do not.

- *Major medical* is a policy that pays the bills for treatment in and out of hospitals.

- *Comprehensive policies* vary, but usually cover medical expenses in and out the hospital. A common type requires a deductible for expenses outside of the hospital while paying full or nearly full cost for expenses incurred in a hospital.

- *Long-term care policies* cover the costs of custodial care in a nursing home or at home.

- *Disability income* insurance policies provide replacement income if you are unable to work because of illness or accident. Generally, the policy will pay a percentage of your income for a specific amount of time.

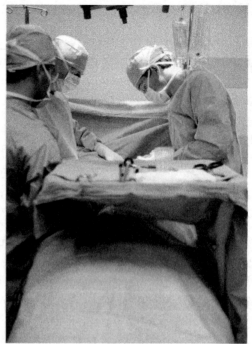

Health insurance covers you if you need surgery.

- *Co-payment* insurance policies are where you pay an amount of $10 or $15 at the time of your appointment or service and the insurance company pays the balance.

Life insurance is one of those things people don't like to think or talk about, but ignoring it could lead to severe financial consequences in the future. The basic types of plans available are:

- *Term insurance* is the type where you are covered for a specific amount of money for a specific length of time, usually one, five, or ten years. If you die during that time period and the premiums are paid, your **beneficiaries** receive the value of the policy. This is the least expensive plan.

- *Whole life insurance* is also called straight life or permanent life. This type of policy has a fixed death benefit and a fixed premium. Part of your premium goes toward insurance coverage and part toward a tax-deferred cash reserve in your name, which is invested by the insurance company. If you cancel the policy, you receive its cash value.

- *Universal life insurance* and *variable life insurance* are similar to whole life insurance. They differ in premium/investment distribution and choices.

It pays to shop around and compare premiums and levels of insurance. The cost of your insurance premiums will be reduced if you raise the deductible on the policy.

Answer the following questions.

2.63   Why is having insurance important to your overall financial plan? _____

_____

2.64   What is the difference between a claim and a premium? _____

_____

2.65   Why should you have liability insurance on your car? _____

_____

Answer *true* **or** *false*.

2.66   _____   Your homeowner's insurance covers all your personal possessions for up to 50%
                        of the amount of insurance on the building.

2.67   _____   Group health insurance is more expensive than individual health insurance.

2.68   _____   Whole life insurance has fixed death benefits and a fixed premium.

INCOME TAX

Figuring your income tax requires four steps.

1.   Add up your total income such as wages, interest, and dividends.

2.   Subtract your deductions: the result is your taxable income. There are four types of deductions:

     a.   Business deductions are for those who own their own business.
     b.   Adjustments are a special class of deductions you are allowed to claim even if you don't claim
          itemized deductions. You claim your deductions at the bottom of page 1 of Form 1040. An exam-
          ple of an adjustment deduction would be student loan interest. When you subtract your adjust-
          ments from the total income, you arrive at an important number called *adjusted gross income*.
          On Form 1040, that's the last number on page 1 and also the number at the top of page 2.
     c.   Itemized deductions; standard deduction. Each year you are allowed to claim itemized deduc-
          tions or the standard deduction, whichever is larger. Itemized deductions include such items
          as medical expenses, state and local taxes, mortgage interest, and investment expenses. If
          those items don't add up to a large enough total, you claim the standard deduction instead.
          Most people find that the standard deduction is larger than their itemized deductions, at least
          until they become homeowners. As your income grows, your itemized deductions will most
          likely grow as well. When they become large enough you should claim itemized deductions
          instead of the standard deduction.
     d.   Exemptions. You are allowed a deduction just for being you: a personal exemption. You are also
          allowed an exemption for each person who qualifies as your **dependent**.

3.   Apply the tax rates to find your tax. Once you know your taxable income, you apply the tax rates
     to find out your tax. You can do this simply by looking up your taxable income in a table supplied
     with your tax form.

4.   Subtract your withholding and other payments and credits: the result is the tax you owe or the
     refund you have coming.

It is possible for most of us to save the necessary documents and prepare our own income tax returns. Some of the most important forms include:

Form 1040. This is the master form you complete when you file your tax return. Filling one out could require you to file additional forms and schedules. 1040EZ and 1040A are shorter versions of 1040 for less complicated returns.

Form **1040** Department of the Treasury—Internal Revenue Service

U.S. Individual Income Tax Return 2008 (99) IRS Use Only—Do not write or staple in this space.

For the year Jan. 1–Dec. 31, 2008, or other tax year beginning , 2008, ending , 20

OMB No. 1545-0074

Label (See instructions on page 14.) **Use the IRS label.** Otherwise, please print or type.

L A B E L H E R E

Your first name and initial | Last name | Your social security number

If a joint return, spouse's first name and initial | Last name | Spouse's social security number

Home address (number and street). If you have a P.O. box, see page 14. | Apt. no.

City, town or post office, state, and ZIP code. If you have a foreign address, see page 14.

▲ You **must** enter your SSN(s) above. ▲

Checking a box below will not change your tax or refund.

Presidential Election Campaign ▶ Check here if you, or your spouse if filing jointly, want $3 to go to this fund (see page 14) ▶ ☐ You ☐ Spouse

Filing Status
Check only one box.

1 ☐ Single
2 ☐ Married filing jointly (even if only one had income)
3 ☐ Married filing separately. Enter spouse's SSN above and full name here. ▶
4 ☐ Head of household (with qualifying person). (See page 15.) If the qualifying person is a child but not your dependent, enter this child's name here. ▶
5 ☐ Qualifying widow(er) with dependent child (see page 16)

Exemptions

6a ☐ **Yourself.** If someone can claim you as a dependent, **do not** check box 6a
b ☐ **Spouse**

Boxes checked on 6a and 6b
No. of children on 6c who:
• lived with you _____
• did not live with you due to divorce or separation (see page 18) _____
Dependents on 6c not entered above _____
Add numbers on lines above ▶

c Dependents:

(1) First name Last name	(2) Dependent's social security number	(3) Dependent's relationship to you	(4) ✓ if qualifying child for child tax credit (see page 17)
			☐
			☐
			☐
			☐

If more than four dependents, see page 17.

d Total number of exemptions claimed

Income

Attach Form(s) W-2 here. Also attach Forms W-2G and 1099-R if tax was withheld.

If you did not get a W-2, see page 21.

Enclose, but do not attach, any payment. Also, please use **Form 1040-V.**

7 Wages, salaries, tips, etc. Attach Form(s) W-2 | 7
8a **Taxable** interest. Attach Schedule B if required | 8a
b **Tax-exempt** interest. **Do not** include on line 8a | 8b
9a Ordinary dividends. Attach Schedule B if required | 9a
b Qualified dividends (see page 21) | 9b
10 Taxable refunds, credits, or offsets of state and local income taxes (see page 22) | 10
11 Alimony received | 11
12 Business income or (loss). Attach Schedule C or C-EZ | 12
13 Capital gain or (loss). Attach Schedule D if required. If not required, check here ▶ ☐ | 13
14 Other gains or (losses). Attach Form 4797 | 14
15a IRA distributions | 15a | b Taxable amount (see page 23) | 15b
16a Pensions and annuities | 16a | b Taxable amount (see page 24) | 16b
17 Rental real estate, royalties, partnerships, S corporations, trusts, etc. Attach Schedule E | 17
18 Farm income or (loss). Attach Schedule F | 18
19 Unemployment compensation | 19
20a Social security benefits | 20a | b Taxable amount (see page 26) | 20b
21 Other income. List type and amount (see page 28) ____ | 21
22 Add the amounts in the far right column for lines 7 through 21. This is your **total income** ▶ | 22

Adjusted Gross Income

23 Educator expenses (see page 28) | 23
24 Certain business expenses of reservists, performing artists, and fee-basis government officials. Attach Form 2106 or 2106-EZ | 24
25 Health savings account deduction. Attach Form 8889 | 25
26 Moving expenses. Attach Form 3903 | 26
27 One-half of self-employment tax. Attach Schedule SE | 27
28 Self-employed SEP, SIMPLE, and qualified plans | 28
29 Self-employed health insurance deduction (see page 29) | 29
30 Penalty on early withdrawal of savings | 30
31a Alimony paid b Recipient's SSN ▶ | 31a
32 IRA deduction (see page 30) | 32
33 Student loan interest deduction (see page 33) | 33
34 Tuition and fees deduction. Attach Form 8917 | 34
35 Domestic production activities deduction. Attach Form 8903 | 35
36 Add lines 23 through 31a and 32 through 35 | 36
37 Subtract line 36 from line 22. This is your **adjusted gross income** ▶ | 37

For Disclosure, Privacy Act, and Paperwork Reduction Act Notice, see page 88. Cat. No. 11320B Form **1040** (2008)

38

The Internal Revenue Service (IRS) sends tax packages complete with the most often used forms and preprinted mailing labels every year. If you don't receive one, you can get forms at some malls, registered IRS offices, and the Internet. There are also some easy-to-use computer software programs available for completing your taxes.

Form W-4. The government expects to receive your tax payments throughout the year. If you have a full-time job, you will fill out a W-4 form to determine how much of your pay is withheld in taxes. Your employer then sends your taxes to the government. The W-4 form comes with a worksheet that will help you figure the amount that should be withheld.

Form W-4 (2008)

Purpose. Complete Form W-4 so that your employer can withhold the correct federal income tax from your pay. Consider completing a new Form W-4 each year and when your personal or financial situation changes.

Exemption from withholding. If you are exempt, complete **only** lines 1, 2, 3, 4, and 7 and sign the form to validate it. Your exemption for 2008 expires February 16, 2009. See Pub. 505, Tax Withholding and Estimated Tax.

Note. You cannot claim exemption from withholding if (a) your income exceeds $900 and includes more than $300 of unearned income (for example, interest and dividends) and (b) another person can claim you as a dependent on their tax return.

Basic instructions. If you are not exempt, complete the **Personal Allowances Worksheet** below. The worksheets on page 2 adjust your withholding allowances based on itemized deductions, certain credits, adjustments to income, or two-earner/multiple job situations. Complete all worksheets that apply. However, you may claim fewer (or zero) allowances.

Head of household. Generally, you may claim head of household filing status on your tax return only if you are unmarried and pay more than 50% of the costs of keeping up a home for yourself and your dependent(s) or other qualifying individuals. See Pub. 501, Exemptions, Standard Deduction, and Filing Information, for information.

Tax credits. You can take projected tax credits into account in figuring your allowable number of withholding allowances. Credits for child or dependent care expenses and the child tax credit may be claimed using the **Personal Allowances Worksheet** below. See Pub. 919, How Do I Adjust My Tax Withholding, for information on converting your other credits into withholding allowances.

Nonwage income. If you have a large amount of nonwage income, such as interest or dividends, consider making estimated tax payments using Form 1040-ES, Estimated Tax for Individuals. Otherwise, you may owe additional tax. If you have pension or annuity income, see Pub. 919 to find out if you should adjust your withholding on Form W-4 or W-4P.

Two earners or multiple jobs. If you have a working spouse or more than one job, figure the total number of allowances you are entitled to claim on all jobs using worksheets from only one Form W-4. Your withholding usually will be most accurate when all allowances are claimed on the Form W-4 for the highest paying job and zero allowances are claimed on the others. See Pub. 919 for details.

Nonresident alien. If you are a nonresident alien, see the Instructions for Form 8233 before completing this Form W-4.

Check your withholding. After your Form W-4 takes effect, use Pub. 919 to see how the dollar amount you are having withheld compares to your projected total tax for 2008. See Pub. 919, especially if your earnings exceed $130,000 (Single) or $180,000 (Married).

Personal Allowances Worksheet (Keep for your records.)

A   Enter "1" for **yourself** if no one else can claim you as a dependent . . . . **A** _____

B   Enter "1" if: { • You are single and have only one job; or
• You are married, have only one job, and your spouse does not work; or
• Your wages from a second job or your spouse's wages (or the total of both) are $1,500 or less. } . . **B** _____

C   Enter "1" for your **spouse.** But, you may choose to enter "-0-" if you are married and have either a working spouse or more than one job. (Entering "-0-" may help you avoid having too little tax withheld.) . . . . **C** _____

D   Enter number of **dependents** (other than your spouse or yourself) you will claim on your tax return . . . . . . **D** _____

E   Enter "1" if you will file as **head of household** on your tax return (see conditions under **Head of household** above) . **E** _____

F   Enter "1" if you have at least $1,500 of **child or dependent care expenses** for which you plan to claim a credit . . **F** _____
     (**Note.** Do **not** include child support payments. See Pub. 503, Child and Dependent Care Expenses, for details.)

G   **Child Tax Credit** (including additional child tax credit). See Pub. 972, Child Tax Credit, for more information.
     • If your total income will be less than $58,000 ($86,000 if married), enter "2" for each eligible child.
     • If your total income will be between $58,000 and $84,000 ($86,000 and $119,000 if married), enter "1" for each eligible child plus "1" **additional** if you have 4 or more eligible children.   **G** _____

H   Add lines A through G and enter total here. (**Note.** This may be different from the number of exemptions you claim on your tax return.) ▶ **H** _____

For accuracy, complete all worksheets that apply. { • If you plan to **itemize or claim adjustments to income** and want to reduce your withholding, see the **Deductions and Adjustments Worksheet** on page 2.
• If you have **more than one job** or are **married and you and your spouse both work** and the combined earnings from all jobs exceed $40,000 ($25,000 if married), see the **Two-Earners/Multiple Jobs Worksheet** on page 2 to avoid having too little tax withheld.
• If **neither** of the above situations applies, **stop here** and enter the number from line H on line 5 of Form W-4 below. }

- - - - - - - - - - - - Cut here and give Form W-4 to your employer. Keep the top part for your records. - - - - - - - - - - - -

Form **W-4**	**Employee's Withholding Allowance Certificate**	OMB No. 1545-0074
Department of the Treasury Internal Revenue Service	▶ **Whether you are entitled to claim a certain number of allowances or exemption from withholding is subject to review by the IRS. Your employer may be required to send a copy of this form to the IRS.**	2008

1 Type or print your first name and middle initial.	Last name	2 Your social security number

Home address (number and street or rural route)	3 ☐ Single ☐ Married ☐ Married, but withhold at higher Single rate. **Note.** If married, but legally separated, or spouse is a nonresident alien, check the "Single" box.
City or town, state, and ZIP code	4 If your last name differs from that shown on your social security card, check here. You must call 1-800-772-1213 for a replacement card. ▶ ☐

5   Total number of allowances you are claiming (from line **H** above **or** from the applicable worksheet on page 2)   **5** _____

6   Additional amount, if any, you want withheld from each paycheck . . . . **6** $ _____

7   I claim exemption from withholding for 2008, and I certify that I meet **both** of the following conditions for exemption.
     • Last year I had a right to a refund of **all** federal income tax withheld because I had **no** tax liability **and**
     • This year I expect a refund of **all** federal income tax withheld because I expect to have **no** tax liability.
     If you meet both conditions, write "Exempt" here . . . . ▶ **7** _____

Under penalties of perjury, I declare that I have examined this certificate and to the best of my knowledge and belief, it is true, correct, and complete.
Employee's signature
(Form is not valid unless you sign it.) ▶   Date ▶

8 Employer's name and address (Employer: Complete lines 8 and 10 only if sending to the IRS.)	9 Office code (optional)	10 Employer identification number (EIN)

Form W-2. Your employer should send this form to you every January. It lists all the federal taxes you paid during the year as well as state and local taxes that were withheld from your pay. Check it carefully and file it with your tax return.

a Employee's social security number				Safe, accurate, FAST! Use	IRS e-file	Visit the IRS website at www.irs.gov/efile.
b Employer identification number (EIN)		OMB No. 1545-0008		1 Wages, tips, other compensation		2 Federal income tax withheld
c Employer's name, address, and ZIP code				3 Social security wages		4 Social security tax withheld
				5 Medicare wages and tips		6 Medicare tax withheld
				7 Social security tips		8 Allocated tips
d Control number				9 Advance EIC payment		10 Dependent care benefits
e Employee's first name and initial Last name Suff.				11 Nonqualified plans		12a See instructions for box 12
				13 Statutory employee Retirement plan Third-party sick pay		12b
				14 Other		12c
						12d
f Employee's address and ZIP code						

15 State Employer's state ID number	16 State wages, tips, etc.	17 State income tax	18 Local wages, tips, etc.	19 Local income tax	20 Locality name

Form **W-2** Wage and Tax Statement   **2009**   Department of the Treasury—Internal Revenue Service

Copy B—To Be Filed With Employee's FEDERAL Tax Return.
This information is being furnished to the Internal Revenue Service.

Complete the following activities.

2.69   List the four steps required to figure your income tax.

a. _____

_____

b. _____

_____

c. _____

_____

d. _____

_____

2.70   Give an example of an adjustment deduction that you might have. _____

_____

2.71   Which would you most likely use: itemized deductions or the standard deduction? _____

_____

2.72   What is a dependent? _____

2.73   You fill out and give your employer a _____ if you have a full-time job.

2.74   You receive a _____ form from your employer.

2.75   As a teenager you would most likely use a _____ tax form.

Review the material in this section in preparation for the Self Test. This Self Test will check your mastery of this particular section as well as your knowledge of the previous section.

SELF TEST 2

Fill in the blanks (each answer 2 points).

2.01   Forms that answer questions such as Who? What? When? Where? and Why? are called _____ forms.

2.02   Forms that answer questions such as How much? and How many? are called _____.

2.03   A heavy paper folder with pockets for storing papers is called a(n) _____.

2.04   A locked container that resists heat is a(n) _____.

2.05   A locked container within a bank vault is a(n) _____.

2.06   Lists of insurance companies, policy numbers, and amounts should be stored in _____ _____.

2.07   Stock certificates should be stored in _____.

2.08   The type of bank where the members may have the same place of employment is a _____ _____.

2.09   A _____ offers investment services.

2.010   Two retirement financial plans that companies offer are a 401(k) plan and a _____ plan.

2.011   A _____ is an example of long-term credit.

2.012   Which tax form do you fill out and give to your employer if you have a full time job? _____

2.013   A teenager would most likely use the _____ tax form.

2.014   The FDIC insures an account up to $ _____.

Match the terms (each answer, 3 points).

2.015   _____ an order to a bank to pay money

2.016   _____ form listing the checks and money to be put into an account

2.017   _____ should be done to a check before it is deposited

2.018   _____ the monthly record listing the checks, deposits, and charges for an account

2.019   _____ what the bank pays for the use of a depositor's money

2.020   _____ the right to buy something now and pay later

2.021   _____ annual amount you pay for insurance coverage

2.022   _____ request for payment from an insurance company

a. bank statement

b. check

c. claim

d. credit

e. deposit slip

f. endorse

g. interest

h. premium

Answer *true* **or** *false* (each answer, 2 points).

2.023 _____ You should have at least liability insurance on your car.

2.024 _____ Homeowner's insurance covers all your personal possessions for up to 65% of the amount of insurance on the building.

2.025 _____ Group health insurance is more expensive than individual health insurance.

2.026 _____ Whole life insurance has fixed death benefits and a fixed premium.

2.027 _____ A résumé should be only one or two typed pages.

2.028 _____ Collect information beforehand if applying for a job whether it is in a Christian ministry or secular work.

2.029 _____ Looking down or avoiding eye contact indicates to the interviewer that you may have something to hide.

2.030 _____ Dress conservatively for a job interview.

Define the following terms (each answer, 3 points).

2.031 budget _____

2.032 verify _____

2.033 overdrawn _____

2.034 reconciling _____

Short answer (each answer, 4 points).

2.035 How do banks make their money? _____

_____

2.036 Besides a savings account, what are two other options for investing money? _____

_____

2.037 How should church and God fit into our budget? Use scripture to back up your statements. _____

_____

_____

Essay (each answer, 2 points).

2.038 What are the four steps required to figure your income tax?

    a. _____

    b. _____

    c. _____

    d. _____

80 / 100

Score _____

Add Check _____

Initial   Date

43

III. LEGAL MATTERS, FORMS, AND CONTRACTS

Everyone performs a legal transaction of some kind sometime in her life. Not all legal transactions require you to hire a lawyer. One of the most common, one that you might not even think of as a legal transaction, is the purchase of an item. Whether you purchase a soft drink or a new car, the bill of sale (e.g. the receipt) serves as written evidence of the transfer of title from one party to another.

The thought of your own mortality or the mortality of a loved one may be unpleasant—but the thought of everything that you or they have worked so hard for coming under the control of the courts after you or your loved one's death is even harder. Writing your will is only the first step in estate planning. Many people have a living will and a durable power of attorney as well as a will.

Understanding a standard lease agreement will be important for you as a young adult starting out on your own. You may want to lease an apartment or car sometime in the future. Learning the language used in a lease agreement may save you money and unpleasant circumstances in the future.

The last part of this section of LIFEPAC 8 will introduce you to the responsibilities of legal forms such as loans, licenses, insurance, and maintenance involved in purchasing and owning a car.

Section Objectives

Review these objectives. When you have completed this section, you should be able to:

19. Understand the legalities concerning bills of sale.

20. Define the following: wills, living wills, and durable power of attorney.

21. Know your rights concerning lease agreements.

22. Identify the responsibilities and legalities involved in purchasing and owning a car.

BILLS OF SALE

For a major purchase, the bill of sale should contain a detailed description of the item; in the case of a car, boat, or other vehicle, this includes color, make, model, registration number, etc. It should also have the date of transfer from seller to buyer and the signatures of both parties.

The bill of sale does not give the buyer any specific set of rights. To establish these, a sales contract is necessary. You should always have a sales contract when making a big purchase. This contract needs to be signed by both parties also.

Not all sales contracts are created equal. No matter how much you want an item, do not sign anything until you have read and reread it and thoroughly understand every word. Do not rely on a handshake alone. Get all the terms of the agreement *in writing*. Another important thing to know about contracts is to fill in all the blanks. Do not leave any blank spaces; they must either be filled in or crossed out. Protect yourself from someone filling in information for their benefit later, after you have signed the contract. Make sure you understand the payment schedule and that it is included in writing in the contract. Be sure you keep a copy of the contract in a safe place.

Just another reminder; contracts are **legally binding** and once you have signed one, you are obligated to follow through.

Answer the following.

3.1   Define a bill of sale. _____

_____

3.2   Is it legally binding? _____

3.3   What three things should a bill of sale include?

    a.   _____

    b.   _____

    c.   _____

3.4   What should the buyer have to insure specific rights besides the bill of sale? _____

_____

Answer *true* **or** *false.*

3.5   _____   Only fill out the blanks on a sales contract that pertain to your particular sale.

3.6   _____   Sales contracts are legally binding.

WILLS, LIVING WILLS, AND DURABLE POWER OF ATTORNEY

Many people are under the mistaken belief that if they don't have a will that spouses, children, or other family members will automatically inherit everything. This is not necessarily true. Each individual state determines the laws of **intestacy** to determine the distribution of all assets that were solely owned by the **decedent**. This could mean that everything owned by a married decedent will be divided equally between the wife and all children, parents, brothers, sisters, and possibly even nieces and nephews. The courts can even sell your possessions without regard for family heirlooms. To protect the immediate family, spouse and children, a will should be written.

Anyone of legal age who has amassed any funds, property, or possessions should have a will. It should be written as soon as possible. Review your will every two to three years to update any additional or changed information. It should be reviewed even sooner if your economic status has changed considerably.

Your will should be stored in a safe place but accessible to you and, upon your death, to your executor. A safe deposit box is the preferred place to store your will or at least a copy of your will. Be sure you check your state laws concerning the accessibility of a safe deposit box after your death. Some states prohibit opening them after a death until the state tax authorities can review their contents, which would keep the will from the executor. A fireproof box at home would be an appropriate choice for storage. Make sure the executor of your will knows where all important legal documents, including your will, are stored.

Probate is the legal process that involves filing the decedent's will, identifying and accounting assets, paying debts and death taxes, and distributing the remainder as dictated in the terms of the will. The entire process generally takes anywhere from six months to a year and is managed by the will's executor and an attorney.

A will protects the interests of your family.

There are ways to protect your assets, especially your large items such as a home. You can set up living trusts, where a designated trustee (whom you have chosen) will take over the management of your property in your place upon your death. Joint tenancy also protects your assets. It is a type of shared ownership in which the surviving owner automatically inherits your share of the property at the time of your death. Retirement plans, life insurance, and gifts can be set up with designated **beneficiaries**. Whatever method you choose, there are ways to avoid the probate process of the courts.

A "living will," also referred to as a directive to physicians, is really not a will at all because the provisions are carried out while the **signatory** is still alive. A living will directs medical personnel to withhold or withdraw "heroic measures" or life-support equipment if you are suffering from a terminal, irreversible illness and death is **imminent**. Some states do not recognize the validity of a living will, so you will need to verify this for your individual state.

When drawing up your last will and testament, you may also want to take the time to prepare for the possibility that you could become physically or mentally incapacitated and unable to tend to your own medical or financial affairs. The document that addresses this issue is called a durable power of attorney, in which you appoint someone else as your "attorney in fact" to handle your financial affairs and make and manage your health care decisions in the event that you can no longer do so. The document does not take effect until that time.

Answer the following.

3.7   Why is it important to know what the intestacy laws of your state are? _____

_____

3.8   What is the preferred place to store your will? _____

3.9   Define probate. _____

_____

3.10   What are three ways in which you can protect your assets from the probate process?

a. _____

b. _____

c. _____

3.11   What is a living will? _____

_____

3.12   What is the document that gives your attorney the right to handle your financial and medical affairs in the event that you are incapacitated? _____

LEASE AGREEMENTS

Most residential leases have standard language—but you must still read them carefully. Some clauses, such as those concerning pets, may be negotiable. If you and your landlord do agree to any changes, make sure that they are in writing and that the clauses they are replacing are removed or crossed out and initialed by you and your landlord.

Many leases, for example, contain clauses that effectively allow the landlord to postpone your move-in date if the apartment isn't ready on time or if the previous tenants have not moved out yet.

Your lease will probably also contain a clause in which you agree that the apartment is in proper condition. Do not sign until any existing damage such as holes in the wall or repairs, such as replacement of carpets has been completed or a written list of existing damage and repairs has been initialed by both you and your landlord. You do not want to be held liable for damage that existed before you ever saw the place.

The "access to the apartment" clause that allows the landlord access to your apartment for repairs or for showing it as a sample to a prospective tenant, should contain specific language about the hours your landlord can enter your apartment and how much notice you must be given.

Check for clauses regarding late fees: many states have laws governing when and how much they can charge you for late payments.

Check for clauses that affect the "rules and regulations" set up by your landlord. Ask for a written copy of any such rule before you sign your lease.

Never assume that *any* utilities are paid by your landlord. Check carefully to see who is responsible for payment.

There is much to consider when you lease, whether it be an apartment or a car. Be sure to read the contract closely to look for any raised red flags that may be a warning to you about the legality of the lease or any clauses in the lease.

Answer the following questions.

3.13   What are the two most important things you should do before signing any contract? _____

_____

3.14   Why must both you and the landlord initial or sign any changes made in the lease? _____

_____

Answer *true* **or** *false.*

3.15   _____   It is safe to assume that the utilities will be paid by the landlord.

3.16   _____   The "access to the apartment" clause gives the landlord the right to enter your apartment as he wishes and whenever he wishes.

3.17   _____   You can be held liable for any pre-existing damage to the apartment if you sign the lease without noting these damages.

PURCHASING AND OWNING A CAR

When one borrows money for a car, one of the car expenses is the interest paid on the car loan. As a car owner, it is important to keep track of the interest as well as all the other car expenses: car loan and interest, insurance, license and registration, gasoline and oil, repairs, maintenance and tires. Look at how to compute and record each of these expenses.

Car Loan. Buying a car entails making a down payment and taking out a car loan for three to five years. After the loan is paid, it is no longer considered an expense. Often, the down payment money comes from the sale or trade of another car.

If you have a four-year loan with a payment of $140 per month, you can figure your yearly expenses for the loan by multiplying by twelve.

$140 x 12 = $1,680

CAR EXPENSES FOR 20—

Car loan $1,680

48

Insurance. The insurance payment is due quarterly, which means a payment is due four times a year. Each quarter is three months long. The first quarter is January, February, and March and so forth. If each payment is $150: the total is $600 for the year.

INSURANCE $600

License and registration. Other costs are for a driver's license and license plates. There are also local fees in some areas. Let's say you have to pay $50 to the state motor vehicle department for your license plates and $20 for your driver's license—a total of $70 for license and registration.

LICENSES AND REGISTRATION $70

Gas and Oil. Keep careful records of gas expenses if you use your car for your job or are curious about the cost of running a car. Gas is a major cost of operating a car. For the same reason, keep records of all the expenses for oil changes and lubrication. Let's say your yearly gas and oil expenses are $850.

GAS AND OIL $850

Repairs and Tires. For the sake of our chart for recording car expenses for one year, let's say you had the car repaired twice this year and bought new tires.

Repairs, Jan 3	$400
Repairs, July 10	$480
Tires, Nov 7	$300
Total:	$1,180

Add this expense to the list:

CAR EXPENSES FOR 20 —	
Car loan	$1,680
Insurance	$600
License and registration	$70
Gas and oil	$850
Repairs and tires	$1,180
Total	$4,380

Figuring Mileage Costs. With your completed list of car expenses, you can now know the total yearly cost of using your car is $4,380. In addition to listing your expenses, you can keep a record of the number of miles you drive. This is done by recording the **odometer** mileage at the beginning of the year and subtracting it from the mileage at the end of the year.

Odometer mileage, Dec 31	74,627
Odometer mileage, Jan 1	52,414
Total miles for 20—	22,213

To figure the average cost per mile of using your car, you divide the total cost, $4,380, by the number of miles driven, 22,213. $4,380 ÷ 22,213 = $0.20

Your average cost per mile is 20 cents.

Other Car Records. In addition to keeping records of mileage and expenses, you must keep records of other car information. You are responsible for renewing your driver's license and license plates on a regular basis. You must pay your car insurance when it is due, and you must have your car inspected on a regular basis. To insure you don't forget, keep a repair journal including a maintenance schedule and make notes in your calendar to remind yourself.

Purchasing and owning your own car is a big responsibility, but one that can be easily managed if you are willing to organize and keep records accurately. Someday, you will have a number of purchasing and ownership responsibilities to keep records for and can feel confident in your abilities because you have already exercised these techniques of recordkeeping.

Complete these activities.

3.18   Name five kinds of car expenses.

a. _____

b. _____

c. _____

d. _____

e. _____

3.19   To figure the average car cost per mile, divide the total expenses by the total _____

_____

Complete the crossword puzzle.

3.20

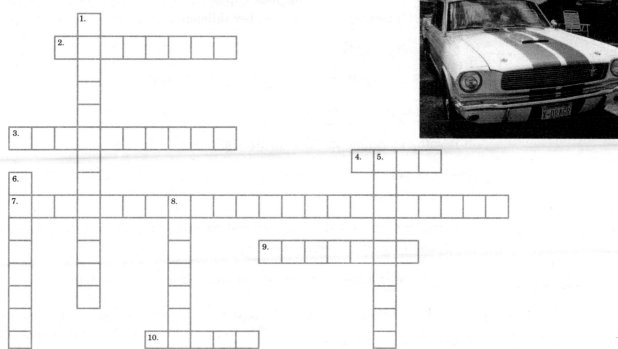

Across:

2. a person who has died
3. directs medical personnel to withhold or withdraw "heroic measures" or life-support
4. a document that states the decedents wishes for the distribution of his/her assets
7. a document that gives legal rights to a designated person to handle your financial affairs and make and manage your health care decisions in the event that you can no longer do so
9. formal permission from a constituted authority to do a specific thing
10. a contract renting land, property to another for a specified period of time and payment

Down:

1. persons designated as the recipients of funds or other property under a will, trust, insurance policy, etc.
5. the state of having not made a will at death
6. an instrument for measuring distances traveled by an automobile
8. the official proving of a will as authentic or valid in a court

---

 Before you take this last Self Test, you may want to do one or more of these self checks.

1. _____ Read the objectives. Determine if you can do them.

2. _____ Restudy the material related to any objectives that you cannot do.

3. _____ Use the SQ3R study procedure to review the material:
   a. **S**can the sections.
   b. **Q**uestion yourself again (review the questions you wrote initially).
   c. **R**ead to answer your questions.
   d. **R**ecite the answers to yourself.
   e. **R**eview areas you didn't understand.

4. _____ Review all vocabulary, activities and Self Tests, writing a correct answer for each wrong answer.

SELF TEST 3

Answer *true* **or** *false* (each answer, 2 points).

3.01 _____ A bill of sale gives the buyer a specific set of rights.

3.02 _____ Contracts are legally binding once they are signed.

3.03 _____ You need to fill in or cross off all blanks on a sales contract.

3.04 _____ It is safe to assume that the utilities will be paid by the landlord.

3.05 _____ The "access to the apartment" gives the landlord the right to enter your
apartment as he wishes and whenever he wishes.

3.06 _____ You can be held liable for any preexisting damage to the apartment if you sign
the lease without noting the damages.

3.07 _____ A functional résumé concentrates on past skills and responsibilities.

3.08 _____ Be early to a job interview.

3.09 _____ Dominate the job interview.

3.010 _____ Your current salary should be written in your résumé.

3.011 _____ The FDIC insures an account up to $100,000.

3.012 _____ Homeowners insurance completely covers the cost of all your possessions as
well as for the building.

3.013 _____ Group health insurance is less expensive than individual health insurance.

3.014 _____ A teenager is more likely to use itemized deductions rather than the standard
deduction when figuring his income tax.

3.015 _____ Whole life insurance has fixed death benefits and a fixed premium.

Fill in the blank (each answer 4 points).

3.016 A bill of sale should include a _____ , _____ , and
_____ .

3.017 A will should be stored in _____ .

3.018 A _____ plan guarantees that the surviving owner automatically inherits
your share of the property at the time of your death.

3.019 A _____-_____ gives your attorney the right to handle your financial
and medical affairs in the event that you are incapacitated.

3.020 Retirement plans, life insurance, and gifts can be set up with designated _____ .

3.021 Forms answering questions such as How much? and How many? are called
_____ forms.

3.022 During a job interview, you will answer questions regarding your education, _____ , and work experience.

3.023 A _____ offers investment services.

Define (each answer 5 points).

3.024 probate _____

_____

3.025 lease _____

_____

Essay (each answer 4 points).

3.026 List five kinds of car expenses.

    a. _____

    b. _____

    c. _____

    d. _____

    e. _____

| 80 / 100 |

Score _____

Adult Check _____

                    Initial   Date

Before taking the LIFEPAC Test, you may want to do one or more of these self checks.

1. _____ Read the objectives. Check to see if you can do them.
2. _____ Restudy the material related to any objectives that you cannot do.
3. _____ Use the SQ3R study procedure to review the material.
4. _____ Review activities, Self Tests, and LIFEPAC vocabulary words.
5. _____ Restudy areas of weakness indicated by the last Self Test.

GLOSSARY

annuity. A specified income payable at stated intervals for a fixed or a contingent period, often for the recipient's life, in consideration of a stipulated premium paid either in prior installment payments or in a single payment.

beneficiary. A person designated to receive funds or other property under a will, trust, insurance policy, etc.

concise. Expressing or covering much in few words.

conscientious. Meticulous, careful.

decedent. A deceased person; no longer living.

dependent. Depending on someone or something else for aid, support, etc.

depositor. One who makes a deposit of money in a bank or similar institution.

dispel. To drive off in various directions: scatter, disperse, dissipate.

gesticulate. To make or use gestures, esp. in an animated or excited manner with or instead of speech.

imminent. Likely to occur at any moment.

intestacy. The state of having not made a will at death.

lease. A contract renting land, buildings, etc, to another for a specified period of time and payment.

legally binding. To put under legal obligation.

maturity. The state of being due; the time when a note or a bill of exchange becomes due.

odometer. An instrument for measuring distance traveled, such as on an automobile.

payee. A person to whom money is paid.

poise. Dignified, self-confident manner or bearing.

rapport. A harmonious or sympathetic relation or connection.

reader friendly. A document written in a universal language, making it easy to read and understand by most people.

reconciling. All the checks written and fees applied to the account within a given month have been subtracted. The deposits have been added. The resulting check register balance and the bank statement balance agree. This process is called reconciling.

register. A check register is a book of forms that provides space for writing in the dates, amounts, and payees for all checks.

segues. To continue at once with the next section without a break.

signatory. Having signed or joined in signing a document.

verify. The process of checking information for completeness and accuracy.

BIBLIOGRAPHY

Beatty, Richard H., *The Five Minute Interview*, John Wiley and Sons, Inc., NY, 1986.

Stewart, Jeffrey R., Daisy L. and Harry, *Financial Management and Record Keeping*, McMillan/McGraw Hill, NY, 1994.

Thomas, Kaye A., *Consider Your Options*, Fairmark Press Inc., ILL, 1999.

Wessinger, Joanna, *The Home Management Book*, Harper Collins Pub., NY, 1995.

Yate, Martin, *Knock 'Em Dead 1997*, Adams Media Corporation, MA, 1997.

55